Secret Keeper Girl

Pajama Party!

Dannah Gresh

HARVEST HOUSE PUBLISHERS
EUGENE, OREGON

Cover and interior design by www.DesignbyJulia.com, Woodland Park, Colorado
Cover illustration by www.DesignbyJulia.com
Interior photos: Steve Tressler, Mountainview Studios, pages 9, 16, 21, 30, 33, 40, 53, 55, 56, 57, 58, 59, 60, 61.
© Shutterstock photographers: Blend Images, page 19; Creatista, page 27; Mat Hayward, pages 29 & 43; Jacek Chabraszewski, page 31; Luis Louro, page 37; Monkey Business Images, page 45 and Boguslawa Koziarska, page 49.
Interior illustrations/spot illustrations by www.DesignbyJulia.com; © Shutterstock artists: Sanqunetti Design; BooHoo; olillia; Lorelyn Medina; and © Jupiter Images.

SECRET KEEPER GIRL is a registered trademark of Dannah Gresh.

SECRET KEEPER GIRL® PAJAMA PARTY
Copyright © 2014 by Dannah Gresh
Published by Harvest House Publishers
Eugene, Oregon 97402
www.harvesthousepublishers.com

ISBN 978-0-7369-6002-1

Printed in China

14 15 16 17 18 19 20 21 22 / RDS-DBJ / 10 9 8 7 6 5 4 3 2 1

What's in This Pajama Party Book

Pajama Party #1
Princesses & Peasants
Have a Royal Ball! ♥ 7

Pajama Party #2
A Purple Pajama Party
Pass the Pillow! ♥ 17

Pajama Party #3
A Spa Party
Spin Your Nail Polish (Huh?) ♥ 35

Pajama Party #4
A Fashion Show
. . . Where You're the Model! ♥ 47

Dedicated to all the moms who sacrifice sleep
to let their girls have "sleep"-overs.

A note to mom

 In recent years, slumber parties have come under the scrutiny of discerning moms. And for good reason: many times these parties are not well supervised, leaving the girls vulnerable to unfiltered Internet access and Netflix selections that you hope your daughter will never watch! (I write about this in more detail in my book *Six Ways to Keep the "Little" in Your Girl*.)

There are three reasonable responses to this.

One is to have a "no sleepover" policy. I've had friends adopt this, and their daughters survive quite well despite what everyone around them says.

The second is to let your daughter go to sleepovers only at homes where you know the family well and have confidence that what the girls will be doing is safe and morally appropriate. This policy is something I suggest you ease into when your daughter is 10, 11, or 12.

But I think the best option is to be the host home. This book makes that easy and sets you up to do just that, but even if you're a "no sleepover" mom, you can host a "pajama party." (Yep, I selected that title carefully.) And your younger daughters will love the thrill of having friends over in their jammies even if the party ends before the sunset.

Want to really up the ante? Invite the girls *and* their moms for some great girl gab!

And enjoy your daughters!

Dannah

Getting Serious with Pajama-Party Planning

I s it possible to make your next pajama* party even more fun than the last one? You bet! You hold in your hands everything you need to host four of your own themed pajama parties.

There are two things that are going to make your parties different from all the rest: your mom and God. That's right—this is one slumber party with two special guests.

You'll enjoy some of the best-ever games, crafts, and recipes, but you'll also get cool, God-driven, Mom-directed story time and girl talk.

Now here's the thing: don't make your mom do all the work. Girl, this book has everything you need to get your party-planning skillz on! Here's your ultimate pajama-party-planning checklist:

 ## One Month Out

1. **Select a party plan.** This book has four to choose from—Princesses & Peasants, the Purple Pajama Party, the Spa Party, and the Fashion Show. (If you want to do all of them, I suggest doing them in order.)

2. **Write a list of friends to invite.** Keep it small so you enjoy yourself. I recommend four to six friends.

---

* Just because you're in your jammies doesn't mean you have to sleep over. That's up to you!

3. Send out invitations. After your mom approves your list, send out invitations with the date, time, place, and a way for them to RSVP. (That's French for *répondez s'il vous plaît*, and it means "please respond." Don't ask me why we use French words on invitations. I don't know!)

 ## One Week Out

1. Write it down. Since you might use my party ideas or add some of your own, you'll want to make a game plan. Putting it on paper ensures that you don't forget to buy something you need. What you write down should include your schedule (what happens and when it happens) and what items you need (basically your shopping list).

2. Go shopping. Ask your mom to take you to the store well in advance so you're not too tired to do all the work it'll take to pull off your shindig. (That's another one of those strange party words. It's not French, but it's odd!)

 ## One Day Out

1. Bake, cook, organize, decorate. Do as much of this as you can at least a day in advance. It makes the day of the party easier, and you won't be too tired to host.

 ## The Day Of

1. Have a pajama party. Enjoy!

Princesses & Peasants
Have a Royal Ball!

Get your girly glam on with tiaras and all-things-pink, or roll it out medieval style with knights and castles. You choose how to theme and decorate your party. I'll give you all the snack recipes, games, and content that you need for a trip back to "once upon a time."

...SECRET....KEEPER.....GIRL! SKG

Invitation Inspiration!

Use parchment paper to write a royal proclamation of festivities. Roll each invitation like a scroll and tie it with a ribbon. (Remember to tell your friends to wear their princess or peasant jammies if they want!)

wear your jammies!

Yummy Recipes!

Secret Keeper Girl Princess-Pink Popcorn

You'll need

- ♥ 4 large bags of popped corn
- ♥ 2 cups sugar
- ♥ 1/2 small box red Jell-O gelatin powder (you pick the flavor!)
- ♥ 1/2 cup water
- ♥ 1 tablespoon butter
- ♥ 1 teaspoon vanilla
- ♥ 1/4 teaspoon baking soda

Put the popped popcorn in a large bowl. Preheat the oven to 250 degrees. Line one or two rimmed baking sheets with foil.

In a medium saucepan (with room for the mixture to at least double in size), bring the sugar, Jell-O, water, and butter to a boil. Once the mixture is fully boiling, cook for 4 minutes without stirring, swirling the pan occasionally. Remove from the heat and stir in the vanilla and soda. Pour over the popcorn and toss with tongs to coat completely.

Spread out onto the baking sheets and bake, stirring once or twice, for an hour. Set aside to cool; break into chunks. Makes about 16 cups.

YUM!

YUM!

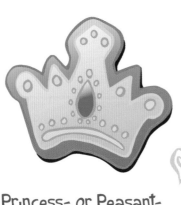

Princess- or Peasant-Themed Cookies

This one is both a recipe for yummy food and a craft to do at the party. Bake sugar cookies in a variety of shapes that fit your chosen theme. For a princess theme, you can make tiaras, glass slippers, scepters, ball gowns, and so on. For a peasant-themed party, you can make castles, crowns, shields, knights, and so on. Provide your guests with a variety of colored icings, small candies, and sprinkles. Let them decorate their cookies.

decorate some fun!

Scepter Berries

You'll need

- ♥ large strawberries with stems
- ♥ white chocolate (such as Nestle Premier White Morsels or Wilton White Candy Melts; 1 cup of pieces will coat about 12 strawberries)
- ♥ red food coloring
- ♥ decorating sugar (sprinkles also work well)

Rinse the berries, then pat them dry with paper towels. Place the white chocolate in a bowl and melt it in the microwave according to the package instructions. Stir in red food coloring until the chocolate is tinted pink (5 drops for 1 cup of chocolate). Dip each strawberry in the chocolate.

Have a Royal Ball

Okay, game time at this party is going to be a ball—a royal ball! (But in PJ's instead of gowns. Why not?)

You'll need

♥ balloons

♥ a royal scepter for each girl

Cover the floor of one room in balloons that you've blown up with regular air, not helium. Hand each girl a royal scepter. (You can buy these or make them as a craft at the party. Just use paper towel tubes, construction paper, glitter, and stickers for a fun project.) Play some fun—maybe princess- or knight-themed—music. You can make this a group challenge and just have everyone keep the balloons in the air until they're tired of it. Or, make it a contest and assign one balloon to each girl. When hers touches the ground, she's out. The last one with her balloon in the air is knighted or crowned princess!

Mom's Story Time

Ask your mom to read this to you and your friends. She's going to ask you to blow your "trumpets" every time she says the word *royal*. You should make your trumpet make this sound: "da-da-taaaa!" It makes the story very silly and much more fun to do it this way. Trust me!

 You'll need

♥ this book

♥ a "trumpet" for each girl (could be a plastic trumpet or a kazoo—or just use your hands to make a pretend trumpet)

da-da-taaaaa!

There once was a Prince who was quite royal. (*Pause for* "da-da-taaaa!") He lived in a glorious castle, which was also quite royal. (*Pause for* "da-da-taaaa!") The castle was high on a mountaintop where birds sang. Rushing rivers raced down the mountainside below, which was covered in acres and acres of flowers.

Now the Prince had many, many servants and soldiers at his side. They were also quite royal! (*Pause for* "da-da-taaaa!")

This Prince had everything! It was a wonderful life, and it was very royal! (*Pause for* "**da-da-taaaa!**")

And yet each day he would take a walk along the mountain ridge, gazing down into the valley with one hope. The hope that he would catch a glimpse of one poor and simple maiden. You see, the Prince saw beyond the simplicity of this little maiden. He saw her beauty. In fact he was absolutely *enthralled* by how beautiful she was. Each day the Prince would return and gaze upon her beauty. He loved her. And he deeply desired to be loved by her in return.

The King was witness to all of this. He knew that, as things were, it was impossible for the Prince to be loved by the simple maiden. He knew, having

much wisdom from his years as King, that it could never work—the Prince being so powerful and royal. (*Pause for "da-da-taaaa!"*) And she, being so simple, and far, far away. He thought to himself, *If I command her to come to the castle, the Prince will always wonder, "Does she really love me or is she simply obeying me?"* Then the King thought, *If I send my horses and guards and soldiers and banners into her world in a grand procession, the Prince will always wonder, "Does she truly love me or is she simply afraid of me?"*

After all, it was all so very royal. (*Pause for "da-da-taaaa!"*)

The King pondered this at great length, until finally he had a magnificent idea and whispered it into the ear of his Son. Upon hearing the plan, the Prince was very burdened by the great risk of it all…but the thought of being loved by the maiden was worth any risk. The Prince bowed before the King. The King decreed that from here on his Son would not say anything or do anything that a Prince would say or do.

The Prince then took off his crown, he took off his robes, he took off his princely garments. He instead put upon his body the clothes of his poorest servant. The Father and Son embraced, knowing they were to be separated while the Prince pursued his love. The once wealthy Prince would now go live in the peasant village as the poorest of the poor. And so, he went down into the village to be near the one who had captured his heart…to see if she would love him back.

 The End.

Or is it? Of course, the story is hardly finished. But that's how it was written. To be an open-ended parable or story to get us thinking about something really important!

I've got news for you. That story is *real*. The King represents God the Father. The Prince represents Jesus. And the beautiful peasant girl is *you*. Psalm 45 is a wedding song, which Bible scholars believe portrays the love God has for us. In verse 11 he says, "Let the king be enthralled by your beauty." In verse 13, he actually calls you a princess. Here's how the verses go:

"Let the king be enthralled by your beauty…all glorious is the princess within her chamber."

Psalm 45:11a, 13a

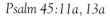

Pillow Talk with Mom

Spend ten minutes discussing the story. What are the girls' favorite parts? How is the King like God? How is the Prince like Jesus? Why do you think the story ends with the Prince coming down from the mountaintop—and we don't know if the girl chooses to love him or not? (You might talk about how we have to choose to love Jesus.)

Note to Mom: This story adapts a widely used parable from Søren Kierkegaard's *Philosophical Fragments*. It's used in the Secret Keeper Girl Pajama Party Tour. Order the DVD of this live show if you'd like one of our talented teachers to deliver the teaching rather than telling the story yourself.

Popcorn Prayer

Before the night ends, offer up some "popcorn prayers." Each girl quickly "pops up" one or two sentences to God.

A Purple Pajama Party
Pass the Pillow!

*This party is all about the pajamas…and the beloved color purple!
Invite your friends to wear their fuzzy slippers and their footie jammies
or their rainbow socks with a pajama gown. Doesn't matter what kind
of jammies, just so they're ready to celebrate girl-style!*

SECRET ···· KEEPER ···· GIRL!

SKG

Secret Keeper GiRL

Invitation Inspiration!

Make a super-cute purple pillow cover to send as an invitation to your friends!

You'll need

- ♥ 1 purple pillow cover for each girl you're inviting (get them cheap at a dollar store!)
- ♥ 1 free downloadable Secret Keeper Girl Pillow Case art (from secretkeepergirl.com)
- ♥ 1 sheet of Avery iron-on transfer paper for each girl
- ♥ 1 safety pin for each girl
- ♥ 1 sheet of paper to write the details of the party
- ♥ purple pens

First, download your Secret Keeper Girl Pillow Case art and the instructions from my website. Go to secretkeeper girl.com and look for our 8 Great Dates page. Click on it. Then, click on the pink book cover with the title *8 Great Dates: Talking with Your Daughter About Best Friends and Mean Girls*. When you get to the next page, scroll down until you see "Secret Keeper Girl Pillow Case Art." Download and print this onto Avery iron-on transfer papers. Using the instructions on your Avery iron-on packaging, create a pillow case for each girl you want to invite.

Use the purple pens to write out the details of your party (time, location, what to bring and wear, RSVP info, and so on). Then use the safety pins to tack this to each of the pillow cases.

You can deliver the invitations in person or you can mail them, but if you mail them you'll need big padded mailing envelopes.

Yummy Recipes!

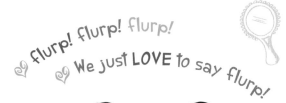

flurp! flurp! flurp!

We just LOVE to say flurp!

Secret Keeper Girl Purple Flurp

This recipe is featured in one of our Secret Keeper Girl fiction books, Danika's Totally Terrible Toss, and is something my mom invented!

You'll need

- ♥ 1 can of crushed pineapple
- ♥ 1 can of blueberry pie filling
- ♥ 1 can sweetened condensed milk
- ♥ 1 8-ounce tub of Cool Whip

Mix the three canned items together the night before your party and refrigerate them overnight.

Add the tub of Cool Whip right before you serve it to all your friends.

FLURP!

Purple Layer Cake

You'll need

- ♥ 1 package white cake mix
- ♥ red food coloring
- ♥ blue food coloring
- ♥ 1 tub of white cake icing

Mix the cake mix according to package directions. Divide it evenly into four bowls. Set one bowl aside because you're going to leave it white.

Add red and blue food coloring to the other three bowls, taking care to make one very dark purple, one medium-purple, and one very light purple. This can be done simply by changing how much food coloring you use. Use more for a darker color. Use less for a lighter color.

Pour the batter into four 9-inch round pans. Bake according to package directions. After they're baked, let the cakes cool.

When they are room temperature, layer your cakes with white icing between them and then ice the entire cake in white. When your friends help you cut the cake, the inside is a wonderful world of purple surprise!

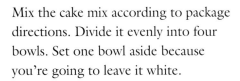

Frozen Grapes

You'll need

♥ 1 container of purple grapes

Rinse the grapes, then pat them dry with paper towels. Line a baking sheet with paper towels and place the grapes on top of the paper towels, leaving space between the grapes. Freeze overnight.

When you bite into them it's like a sweet, yummy grape sorbet! (Don't let them thaw out. They get real mushy!)

freeze up some fun!

Pajama-Party Pillow Pass

Okay, game time at this party is super simple but lots of fun.

You'll need

♥ a pillow (and it'd be great if it's inside one of the purple pillow cases you made for invitations!)

♥ fun, upbeat music from your favorite Christian-music artist

♥ optional: purple candy

Pillow Pass is like "hot potato." Have all your friends sit in a circle. Assign one person to start and stop the music at random. (This person, as in all classic "hot-potato"-type games, can't look at the circle while the game is going on.) When the music starts, pass the pillow around the circle as fast as possible. When the music stops, the girl left holding the pillow is out (which means they become an official cheerleader for the remaining girls!). Play until there's a winner. (The winner gets purple candy.)

23

Guess Who?

This game should be played right before Mom's Story Time.

You'll need

- ♥ name tags
- ♥ purple markers

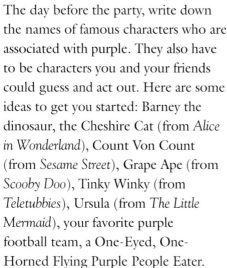

The day before the party, write down the names of famous characters who are associated with purple. They also have to be characters you and your friends could guess and act out. Here are some ideas to get you started: Barney the dinosaur, the Cheshire Cat (from *Alice in Wonderland*), Count Von Count (from *Sesame Street*), Grape Ape (from *Scooby Doo*), Tinky Winky (from *Teletubbies*), Ursula (from *The Little Mermaid*), your favorite purple football team, a One-Eyed, One-Horned Flying Purple People Eater.

Write a different character on each name badge. (Make sure you have enough for everyone!) When it's time for the game, peel off the backing and stick a name badge on each guest's back. Have the girls mingle and try to find out who or what they're supposed to be based on how other guests socialize with them. Girls can ask "yes" or "no" questions to figure out what's written on their label.

 Ask your mom to read this to you and your friends. Your mom is going to need to get her PJ's on for this great story. And she'll also need a few labels to put on them. You can help her by preparing these things.

ugly

unlovable

stupid

You'll need

- ♥ this book
- ♥ pajamas for your mom
- ♥ six name-tag labels for your mom with these words on them: *ugly, unlovable, stupid, perfectly crafted!, loved by God!, empowered by God!*
- ♥ two blank name tags for every girl
- ♥ markers

26

(*Mom comes out wearing her pajamas and three labels on the front reading: "ugly," "unlovable," and "stupid."*)

Do you think my PJ's are funny? Ya know, a funny thing happened at some of the pajama parties I went to when I was your age. I came out looking…well, like this. Covered in "labels." Let me explain:

(*Mom should tell a brief personal testimony about her life. At some point it needs to tie into the labels on her. She can share about a time when she felt ugly, unlovable, or stupid.*)

she's smarter

she's prettier

she has more clothes

she's more fun

I want you to take a look around you right now. You will see girls you think are more beautiful than you, girls who looker taller or smaller, girls who seem to be totally more confident than you… but here is the reality: every one of us has bad thoughts about ourselves. And if we think the same thing again and again, eventually we start to wear invisible labels. Maybe your label would be "unpopular" or "too tall."

I don't know what bad thoughts you have had about yourself, but I want you to know something: God is tickled silly pink, madly in love with you. Psalm 45:11 says, "Let the king be enthralled by your beauty." That's truth. Do you know how I know it is true and what you feel isn't true? Because the Bible says, "God is not a human that he should lie." But…here's the key…you have to be reading the Bible to recognize the difference between truth and lies. Let me show you how it works. The Bible says this in Psalm 139:14a:

"I praise you because I am fearfully and wonderfully made."

G od is tickled silly pink, madly in love with you!

God's Word says that every part of me is made wonderfully by God. That doesn't sound like "ugly" to me. No—

I'm "perfectly crafted!"...

(At this, Mom dramatically rips off "ugly" and replaces it with the label that reads "perfectly crafted!")

perfectly crafted!

This lie says "unlovable." Let's see what God's truth says about that in Jeremiah 31:3b:

> *"I have loved you*
> *with an everlasting love;*
> *I have drawn you with*
> *unfailing kindness."*

God *loves* me! His love is everlasting! I am lovable because God says so. **YOU are lovable because God says so**…(*At this, Mom dramatically rips off "unlovable" to reveal "loved by God!"*)

loved by God!

Oh man, I am feeling free! Okay—one more label. Let's see. "Stupid." The bad word. The one we aren't really supposed to say. But I'm just saying it so we can learn. Hmmm. I have to say, I didn't get the *best* grades in my sixth-grade class (*or Mom says something truthful and similar*). How could God's Word answer that one? Let's look at 2 Corinthians 12:9:

"My grace is sufficient for you, for my power is made perfect in weakness."

empowered by God!

Hmmm? What does this say about me feeling "stupid"? I think it means that I don't have to be the smartest girl in any class. In fact, when I am weak, God is strong. He'll use me no matter what. (*At this, Mom rips off "stupid" to reveal "empowered by God!"*)

I'm free! Did you hear that? *Really* hear that? *You* are

♥ perfectly crafted!

♥ loved by God!

♥ empowered by God!

And that's just the *beginning* of God's thoughts about you recorded in the Bible!

Do you have any labels on you? Maybe you feel "fat" or "short" or like you have "no friends." Let me tell you something. Those labels are *lies!* And the only way to overcome them is to listen to *God's* thoughts about you as recorded in the Bible. Close your eyes and think hard. Ask yourself, **"What is my label?"**

I'm free!

Okay, if you have one I want you to come get one of these paper labels and write your "label" on it.

Just sit and wait there for a moment and really, really, really, really pray. Ask God to take this label...this lie... and rip it off you with his truth. I'm going to come read your label, and together we're going to see if we can find a Bible verse that says something more truthful about you.

hmmm...what is my label?

Pillow Talk with Mom

Spend ten minutes (or more if needed) helping the girls discover God's truth for them. As you do, take their bad label off and replace it with one that says something true. Then, talk about how everyone feels. Have you ever looked around at other people and thought they were better than you? Does anyone want to share what their bad label was and what their new truth is?

Note to Mom: We used this story in the Secret Keeper Girl Pajama Party Tour. Order the DVD of this live show if you'd like one of our talented teachers to deliver the teaching rather than telling the story yourself.

Popcorn Prayer

Before the night ends, offer up some "popcorn prayers." Each girl quickly "pops up" one or two sentences to God.

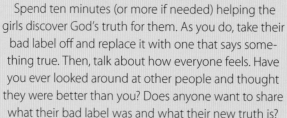

A Spa Party
Spin Your Nail Polish (Huh?)

*This party involves fuzzy bathrobes and facials and manicures!
But don't let beauty treatments fool you—this party is all about
making your inside beautiful!*

Invitation Inspiration!

you are invited!

Use construction paper to cut out an eye-mask-shaped invitation (or buy cheap ones at a dollar store). Decorate the front to be cute and colorful and use the back to write out your invitation. Use a paper hole punch to put two holes on the opposite ends of the eye mask and put a string on it so your friends can bring it with them for an activity you'll do together. (Make sure you remind them on the invitation to bring their eye mask, wear fuzzy bathrobes, and bring one bottle of their favorite nail polish with them.)

Yummy Recipes!

(*And since it's a spa party, all of these yummy treats are also healthy!*)

Body-Cleansing Cucumber Water

This recipe and the Peach Facial below it are from my original Secret Keeper Girl resource, which is now titled 8 Great Dates for Moms and Daughters: How to Talk About True Beauty, Cool Fashion, and…Modesty!

 You'll need

♥ 1 seedless cucumber, thinly sliced

♥ 1 pitcher of ice water

Soak the cucumbers in the pitcher of water for a few hours before you serve it. This releases the cucumber juice into the water. Serve in fun glasses with one cucumber slice on top!

Detoxing Rainbow Fruit Kabobs

You'll need

- ♥ kabob skewers
- ♥ an assortment of firm, colorful, and easy-to-skewer fruit such as strawberries, pineapple chunks, mandarin-orange segments, green grapes, blueberries, black grapes, and so on (the berries will be what makes this a detox treatment that forces bad stuff out of your body)

Create a pattern of color from light to dark when you make your first kabob, such as yellow (pineapple), orange (mandarin segments), green (grapes), red (strawberry), blue (blueberries), and black (black grapes). Follow this pattern for all of the kabobs to give a dramatic effect on your party platter.

kabob! kabob! kabob!

Veggie Cups

You'll need

- ♥ cute mini-cups from a party store or dollar store
- ♥ an assortment of veggies cut into sticks, such as carrots, squash, celery, cucumbers, and zucchini
- ♥ a healthy veggie dip, like hummus, yogurt and dill, or anything else you enjoy that's healthy

Fill the bottom of each little cup with a couple of tablespoons of your favorite dip. Then stick the colorful veggies into the cup until it is packed full and looks adorable!

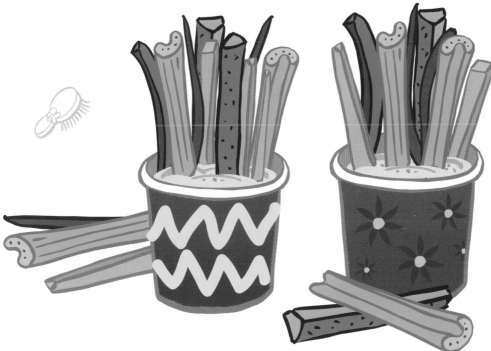

Peach Facial

*I didn't know whether to put this under
yummy foods or games, but since it's
so delicious it ended up under recipes.
Don't eat it all—it's for your face!*

You'll need

- ♥ 1 medium peach per girl
- ♥ 1 tablespoon of cooked oatmeal with
  a little bit of honey per girl
- ♥ two cucumber slices per girl

Cook the peach in a microwave until
it is warm and soft. Then mash it with
a fork. Add enough warm honey and
cooked oatmeal (use package directions)
to make a thick paste. Have each girl
apply it to her skin while it is still warm.

Add cucumber slices to the eye area and
place your eye mask lightly over them
if you'd like. (This is a great chance for
fun photos! But ask each girl first.)

Soak in the yummy aroma for ten
minutes while you all listen to soothing
spa music or nature sounds. Then rinse
your face with cool water.

(Important tip: Don't use this on the
face of someone who has allergies to
the ingredients. You can have a reaction
even if you don't eat it.)

peach facials are a scream!

really? I didn't hear.

Nail Polish Spin

You'll need

♥ to ask each guest to bring a bottle of brightly colored nail polish

Each girl should have a bottle of nail polish. Have the girls make a circle and place their bottles in the middle of their group. Have the first girl spin a bottle of nail polish. Whoever the cap is pointing to when the bottle stops must paint one of her fingernails that color. Then that person spins the next color of nail polish …and so on. Pretty soon everyone has really crazy fingers and toes!

Celebrities Without Makeup

You'll need

♥ pictures of celebs without makeup that you find online

♥ one sheet of paper and a pen for each girl

With your mom's permission or help, get on the Internet and look up photos of various celebrities without makeup! Celebs of any age are fine, but try to find teen and tween celebrities who usually wear a lot of makeup and don't always look the same without it.

During the party, show the pictures to your friends one by one without letting them see the name of the person and let them write down a guess. The person who gets the most correct is the winner. What better gift to give the winner of a spa-party game than a massage? No one to do it, you say? Well, what are friends for? Let each girl take a zone (head, shoulders, feet, hands) and give the winner the massage of her life!

Mom's Story Time

Ask your mom to read this to you and your friends.

A I want you to know something. Every single face we just showed you is a masterpiece created by God. Especially without makeup. We carefully picked these particular stars to showcase because they are, in fact, especially beautiful.

But without their makeup they aren't very recognizable. And sadly, the beauty and fashion industry takes it even further. The photos of stars are altered and perfected using computer programs. Not only do these ladies have crazy amounts of makeup on, but most of the time their photos are digitally changed to impossible perfection.

every face a masterpiece!

So, what does the Bible say about your beauty? Well, it doesn't come from the paint in a makeup kit, that's for sure. How do I know? It says so in the Bible! Let me read you 1 Peter 3:3-4:

"Your beauty should not come from outward adornment, such as elaborate hairstyles and the wearing of gold jewelry or fine clothes. Rather, it should be that of your inner self, the unfading beauty of a gentle and quiet spirit, which is of great worth in God's sight."

Let me say this to you in conversational words. Your beauty won't come from a great haircut, some *fine* jewelry from Claire's, or a fantastic pair of jeans from Justice! Instead, it will show up if you work on making your heart beautiful by being quiet and gentle in the presence of God!

God wants you to feel beautiful. He doesn't say in this verse, "Oh, some of you might be obsessed with beauty and that's really a bummer. But oh…*okay*…here's how you get it!" Instead, God says "*your beauty*" as if it is a fact that you will and should have it! Two things about how you get it:

1 It's not that you can't have a really cute haircut, but that's not what is going to make you *feel* real beauty.

2 True beauty comes from quiet time spent with God. Period!

I have a question for you. Do you spend more time in front of the mirror each day getting your external beauty "on"? Or do you spend more time in quiet time with the Lord, getting your internal beauty "on"?

Today, I want you to make a promise, but only if you want to and really mean it. It's very simple.

"Today, I will spend more time in God's Word than I will in front of the mirror."

making our hearts beautiful!

Pillow Talk with Mom

Spend ten minutes helping the girls discuss how to have daily devotions. You can ask questions like, "Do some of you already read your Bible every day?" "When do you do it?" "Have you ever used a journal or diary to write your prayers to God?" "What are some other ways you can creatively pray?"

Popcorn Prayer

Before the night ends, offer up some "popcorn prayers." Each girl quickly "pops up" one or two sentences to God.

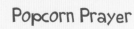

Pajama Party #4

A Fashion Show
...Where You're the Model!

Come in your jammies, but leave in your favorite modest outfit!

...SECRET....KEEPER.....GIRL!

SKG

Invitation Inspiration!

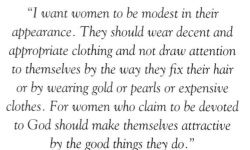

world's cutest invitations!

Go to a local dollar store and buy some funky fabric eyeglass cases. These are going to be your "sleeping bags" for the world's cutest invitations. (If you're really creative, you can sew your own mini sleeping bags.) Print out simple invitations with the details of your big party and slip them into the sleeping bags with the tops peeking out. They'll be extra cute if you can print little faces on the ends that are peeking out the top.

Key Verse

"I want women to be modest in their appearance. They should wear decent and appropriate clothing and not draw attention to themselves by the way they fix their hair or by wearing gold or pearls or expensive clothes. For women who claim to be devoted to God should make themselves attractive by the good things they do."

1 Timothy 2:9-10 (NLT)

Chocolate-Chip Cookie-Dough Dip

You'll need

- ♥ ¼ cup soft butter
- ♥ ¼ cup brown sugar
- ♥ 1 teaspoon vanilla
- ♥ 1 8-ounce tub spreadable cream cheese
- ♥ ¼ cup powdered sugar
- ♥ 1 cup sour cream (optional)
- ♥ ½ cup mini chocolate chips
- ♥ sliced fruit and cookies for dipping

In a small saucepan melt the butter and brown sugar and stir it until it's smooth. Remove it from the heat and add the vanilla. Let it cool.

When the mixture is room temperature, add the rest of the ingredients and mix it up until it's soft. Serve immediately or refrigerate. Serve it with sliced fruit and cookies for dipping.

Mini-Pizza Bar

You'll need

- 💗 1 English muffin or bagel for each girl
- 💗 1 jar pizza sauce
- 💗 1 bag mozzarella cheese
- 💗 your favorite pizza toppings, like pepperoni, pineapple, ham, veggies, and more

This is a do-it-yourself snack. Each girl gets her own English muffin or bagel to cut into two and use to design her own mini pizzas. Just let everyone have fun creating, and then Mom can bake them all together at 350 degrees until the tops are warm and bubbly.

YUM! YUM!

TP Fashion Designers

You'll need

♥ toilet paper!

Divide group into two teams and give each team a roll of toilet paper. Let them pick their models from their teams. Then give the teams two minutes to design an outfit using only toilet paper. Once two minutes are over, pick a winning fashion design and let the models strut the "runway."

Planning Your Secret Keeper Girl Fashion Show

Preselect

- ♥ 3 to 6 models of varying sizes (these should be the friends invited to your pajama party, because *everyone* is in on the runway action!)

- ♥ one outfit for each model (see "How to get the outfits" on next page)

- ♥ MC for fashion show (pick someone fun and outgoing)

- ♥ upbeat Christian music or music without lyrics with "runway" beat

How to pick your own fashion-show outfits. The goal is to use clothes that demonstrate "fashion problems" and show how to fix them emphasizing the Secret Keeper Girl "Truth or Bare Fashion Tests" (included in this chapter). Each outfit should be a different style (sporty, girly, hippie…) to reflect the different tastes of the girl who is wearing it. You can write descriptions for each outfit to have read when the girl modeling it hits your homemade runway.

How to get the outfits. You can do this one of two ways. Go all out and buy or borrow an outfit for each girl, or ask each girl to use the guidelines in this chapter to create or find her own outfit. (You might assign one Truth or Bare Fashion Test to each girl. Although her outfit should pass all the tests, she can show how she had to be extra careful to not fail a test and what solution she offered!)

yeah shopping!

Ideas for problem areas to hit on.

- ♥ see-through blouse or open-knit sweater with a solid T-shirt or tank top underneath
- ♥ the trendy miniskirt paired with leggings or jeans
- ♥ a funky crop top part- nered with a tank top in a complementary color
- ♥ low-rise jeans with a tucked-in tank top underneath the shirt
- ♥ cool, trendy shorts with a 5-inch or 7-inch inseam
- ♥ a sweat suit without words across the bottom
- ♥ a shorter dress to go over jeans that are either skinny or too tight in the rear

Preparation and presentation.

Write up index cards with a description of each outfit. Get the girls all glammed up if you want. Then have the MC (one of the girls or your mom) get the girls all pumped up and in the right frame of mind to have a blast and clap and cheer for each other. Play the music and have the models come down the aisle one at a time as the MC reads the index card about each particular outfit. Encourage the models to have fun with spins and turns!

The Truth or Bare Fashion Tests

Finally, it's time for our nearly world-famous "Truth or Bare Fashion Tests"! Have the models fall into line on the stage. Have fun explaining each test. Have each of the models do the tests on themselves in front of the audience (the other girls), taking time to discuss possible remedies if an outfit fails one of the tests. For some of the tests, you can even have the audience participate. Encourage group participation!

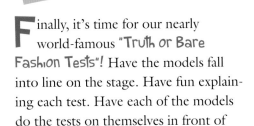

TEST:

 ## Raise & Praise

Target question:
Am I showing too much belly?

Action: Stand straight up and pretend you're going for it in worship, and extend your arms in the air to God. Is this exposing a lot of belly?

Remedy: Go to the guys' department and buy a simple ribbed T-shirt to wear under your funky short T's or with your trendy low-riders. Layers are a great solution to belly shirts.

TEST:

Mirror, Mirror!

Target question:
How short is too short?

Action: Get in front of a full-length mirror. If you are in shorts, sit cross-legged. If you are in a skirt, sit in a chair with your legs crossed. Now, what do you see in that mirror? If you see undies or lots of thigh, your shorts or skirt is too short.

Remedy: Buy longer shorts and skirts!

TEST:

I See London, I See France

Target question:

Can you see my underpants?

Action: Bend over and touch your knees. Have a friend look right at your bottom. Can she see the outline of your underpants or the seams in them? How about the color of them? Can she see your actual underwear because your pants are so low that you're risking a "plumber" exposure? If so, you bomb on this test.

Remedy: Wear white panties with white clothes. If your pants are so tight that you can see the outline of your panties, try buying one size larger.

TEST:

Over & Out

Target question:

Is my shirt too low?

Action: Lean forward a little bit. Can you see too much chest? If so, your shirt is too low.

Remedy: Today's fashions thrive on low-cut shirts. Layering them is often the only remedy. Throw a little T-shirt under a rugby and you have a great look.

Mom's Story Time

Ask your mom to read this to you and your friends.

What does God want us to wear? It's an interesting question, because you might think he doesn't really care. But the Bible says he does.

be a pet shelter friend!

Here's a Bible verse I like a lot:

"I want women to be modest in their appearance. They should wear decent and appropriate clothing and not draw attention to themselves by the way they fix their hair or by wearing gold or pearls or expensive clothes. For women who claim to be devoted to God should make themselves attractive by the good things they do."

1 Timothy 2:9-10 (NLT)

What God wants us to wear goes way deeper than skinny jeans or graphic T's. He wants us to wear beautiful stuff *inside*. Our inner garments are things like kindness, humility, joy, helpfulness. And God-crazy girls wear these beautiful "garments."

God wants you and me to make ourselves attractive by the "good things" we do—like helping your grandma rake her yard or volunteering at a soup kitchen with your mom. I know a few God-crazy girls who are *beautiful* in this way. Like…(*Mom, insert stories about how the girls right in front of you have shown internal beauty. Maybe one of them has been a volunteer at a soup kitchen or another is a great big sister. Try to give an example of how each girl is beautiful.*)

You wear beautiful stuff inside! God's ultimate purpose in 1 Timothy 2:9-10 is to push us into goodness, not to make a lot of rules about our clothes. Right?

But the passage does mention clothes. And it says they should be *appropriate*. Appropriate means "It's okay." Everyone say, "It's okay!" (*Girls say,* "It's okay!") So, let's see if some of these things are appropriate.

Is it OKAY to wear your swimming suit to church?

Naw! We'd look silly!

Is it OKAY to wear an itty-bitty skirt that shows your panties when you bend over to help your friend pick up her books at school?

Naw! That's nasty!

But every day the world is making it "normal" for you and me to be *inappropriate*. And it's not *okay*. *(Pause. Let it sink in.)* Of course, I haven't seen anyone wearing a Speedo to worship, but I've seen plenty of short skirts at school! You know what I'm talking about?

I think the bottom line is this:
God wants nothing about the way we dress to distract from the good things we do for him. That's why he wants us to be careful and modest about how we dress. That's why we like the famous Truth or Bare Fashion Tests. So you can know if an outfit is *okay*!

big sisters are cool!

Pillow Talk with Mom

Spend ten minutes letting each girl share one thing that's beautiful on the *inside* of one of the other girls. Make it a true beauty time of encouragement.

Popcorn Prayer

Before the night ends, offer up some "popcorn prayers." Each girl quickly "pops up" one or two sentences to God.